OH HO HO!
OW
HETIC,
PID
BIT!
ANTINOID EXECUTIVE VILLAINESS HONEY TRAP
UGH!
Sway
SUPERHERO RAPID RABBIT
Thud...
OH DEAR! IT SEEMS YOUR DAYS OF HEROISM ARE OVER.
HM!
BEFORE I KILL YOU, LET'S HAVE A LOOK AT THE FACE BEHIND THAT MASK!

Sparkle
Blush
NGH!
SHE'S TOTALLY MY TYPE!!!

CHAPTER 1 LOVE DOESN'T STOP

ANTI-NOIDS: MYSTERIOUS MONSTERS FROM ANOTHER DIMENSION.
USING THEIR UNIQUE NATURE--THE FACT THAT THE INHABITANTS OF EARTH DON'T RETAIN MEMORIES OF THEM--THEY ADVANCED UPON THE HUMAN WORLD, PLOTTING THE DESTRUCTION OF HUMANITY.

AN INVISIBLE INVASION WAS UNDER-WAY.
IT SEEMED THAT MANKIND HAD MET ITS MATCH AT LAST.

THAT IS, UNTIL A HERO APPEARED, TURNING THE HOPELESS SITUATION AROUND.
THIS HERO'S NAME?

RAPID RABBIT!
THE MYSTERIOUS SUPER-HEROINE HAS FOUGHT BACK FOR MORE THAN HALF A YEAR. SECRET IDENTITY: **UN-KNOWN.** SHE PROTECTS THE MASSES FROM THE ANTINOID MONSTERS, A.K.A. KAIJIN.

STOP RIGHT THERE, ANTI-NOIDS!

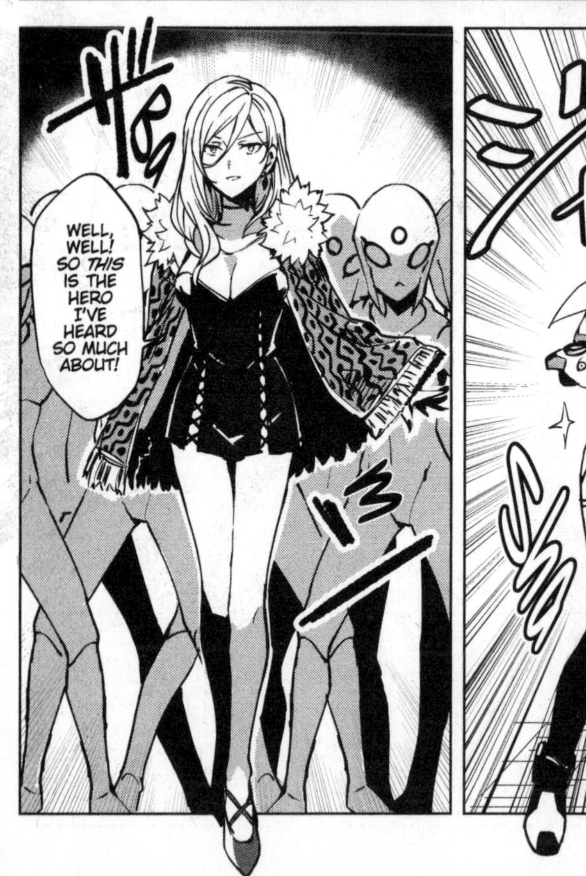

WELL, WELL! SO *THIS* IS THE HERO I'VE HEARD SO MUCH ABOUT!

THIS STOPS NOW!
Bwsh
WHEN VILLAINS ATTACK ...
Voosh
I'LL BE THERE!
Voosh
Voosh
KA-BOOM
I'LL DEFEAT ALL EVIL!
WHY SO MUCH UNNECESSARY POSING?!
AND EXPLOSIONS?!
Staaare
AND YOU, MINIONS! DON'T JUST STAND THERE! ATTACK!
ERM? ARE YOU READY TO START NOW?
AM I READY?! YOU'RE THE ONE WASTING TIME!

ARGH! ENOUGH! GET HER, META WARRIORS !!
OUTTA!
OUTTA!
OUTTAWAY!
KA-BLAM
FWSHHHH

BLAM
BLAM
BLAM
BLAM
BLAM
!
SHFF

FLUTTER
Shuuu
TSK, TSK! YOU THINK THAT JUST BECAUSE YOU TOOK OUT MY MINIONS THAT YOU'RE A MATCH FOR ME?
TAK

THOSE GRUNTS ARE MERELY THE PRELUDE.

YOU SEE, DEAR, THE MAIN ACT OF THE DAY IS ME.
GH!

Ka-Cha
OH HO HO!
DON'T WORRY, MY DEAR. I'LL MAKE THIS SHORT AND SWEET.

FWASH
FSH
SHWA
AAA
I'LL USE MY TRUE POWER AS ONE OF THE ANTINOID EXECUTIVE OFFICERS-- HONEY TRAP!
TP
GYUU
HOW ?!
I TOLD YOU!
IT'S OVER, DAR-LING!

AAAA-
AAAA-
AHHH
!!!
BWOOM

TUNK
WOBBLE

SHUU
THUD

OH DEAR.
LOOKS LIKE HEROES AREN'T ALL THEY'RE CRACKED UP TO BE.
FRANKLY, I'M DISAP-POINTED.
SHWOOO

TP
BUT...

GR
IP
BEFORE I KILL YOU...
YA
LET'S HAVE A LOOK AT THE FACE BEHIND THAT MASK!

GLINT
HUFF!
HUFF!
GL
INT

BLUUUUSH
SHE'S...
TOTALLY MY TYPE!!!

SHLP
FWP
PLOP

I... I CAN'T DO IT! I CAN'T KILL HEEEEER !!!!
BLZOOOM
WHUH?! WH-WHERE ARE YOU GOING?!!

THE NEXT DAY.
DAAAAZE...
AAAAH-HHHHH... I LOVE HER...
Mumble
I WISH WE WERE FRIENDS.
Pluck

URGH! NO, I DO NOT!
A HERO AND A VILLAIN-ESS COULD NEVER GET ALONG.
Toss
Toss

B-BUT ANY-THING'S POSSI-BLE.
Freeze

NO, NO, NO! STOP DREAM-ING!
Pluck
Pluck
Pluck
Pluck
Pluck
Pluck

WHAT ARE YOU DOING, HONEY TRAP?
JOLT
DWUH?!!

WH-WHAT DO *YOU* WANT, MELT OUT?
GOT A MES-SAGE FOR YOU.
OH?

X-SAMA WISHES TO SEE YOU.

FINE. MESSAGE RECEIVED.

IT'S STRANGE, THOUGH.
SHFF...
TO THINK **YOU** OF ALL PEOPLE WOULD COME RUN-NING BACK WITHOUT ELIMINATING THE ENEMY!

HMPH.
THAT'S NONE OF *YOUR* BUSINESS.

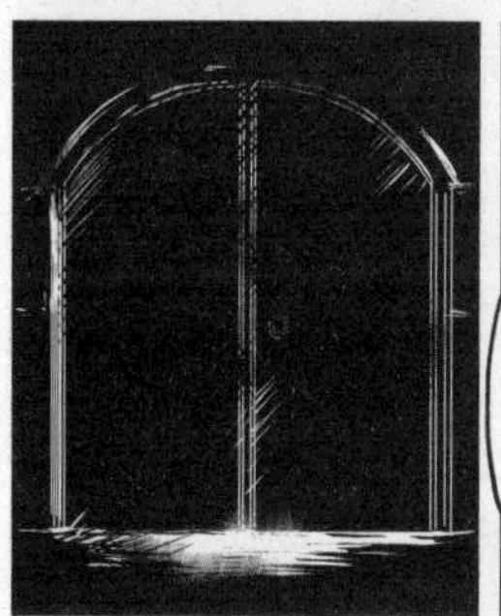

YOU'RE FIRED.
ANTINOID LEADER X

WH-WHAT?! DID I MISHEAR YOU, X-SAMA?!!
I'M FIRED?! JUST LIKE THAT?!
OH, AND I'M SENDING ASSASSINS AFTER YOU LATER. TRY NOT TO DIE~!
YOU MON-STER!!
CAN I AT LEAST GET MY SEVER-ANCE PAY?!

Nope!!!
KER-SLAM

ST-STUPID, EXPLOITATIVE EVIL ORGANIZATION.
GRRR...
I CAN'T BELIEVE THIS! THEY ACTUALLY SENT ASSASSINS AFTER ME!
AND FIRED WITHOUT SEVERANCE PAY?!
I WAS ABLE TO KICK THEIR BUTTS, BUT STILL!
THROB

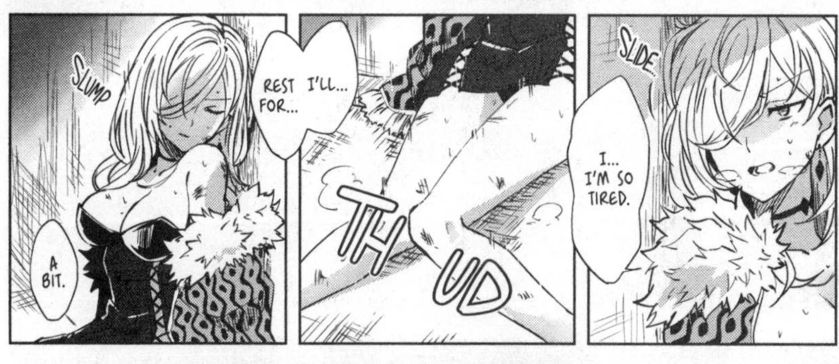
SLIDE
I... I'M SO TIRED.
THUD
I'LL... REST FOR...
SLUMP
A BIT.

Ska
Skuf

NN?
OH!
YOU'RE AWAKE?
?!

WHOA!
VOLT
HELLO, HEART ATTACK.

A-A-A-AREN'T YOU (THE BEAUTY BEHIND) RAPID RABBIT?!
WHY ARE YOU HERE?!!
HAWAH?!

GFF!
RIGHT! SORRY!
YOU WERE PASSED OUT NEAR MY APARTMENT, SO I CARRIED YOU HOME.
YOUR H-HOME?! WAIT, HOLD ON! I'M NOT READY!
NAGIHONO APARTMENTS
READY FOR WHAT?
N-NEVER MIND.

ANYWAY, WHAT HAP-PENED? HOW'D YOU GET THOSE INJURIES?
SHE PATCHED ME UP?
!

WELL...
I WAS LET GO FROM THE ORGANIZA-TION I WAS WORKING FOR.
THEN THEY SENT ASSASSINS TO KILL ME. I MUST HAVE PASSED OUT FROM THE INJURIES...
WAIT.

DO YOU KNOW WHOM YOU'RE TALKING TO?!
RAWR!!
DIDN'T KNOW KAIJIN COULD GET FIRED.

......
YOU'RE HONEY TRAP-SAN.
COR-RECT?

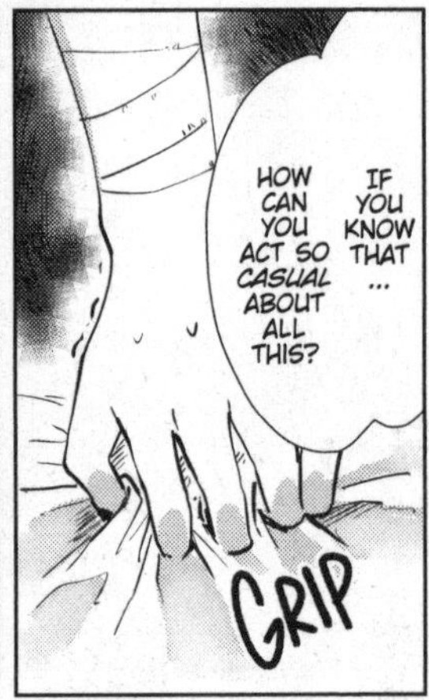
IF YOU KNOW THAT ...
HOW CAN YOU ACT SO *CASUAL* ABOUT ALL THIS?
GRIP

I...I TRIED TO KILL YOU!
......

THAT...
PRESS...
!
DOESN'T MATTER RIGHT NOW.

ENEMY OR ALLY, IF SOME-ONE'S IN TROUBLE, I WANT TO SAVE THEM!
IT'S AS SIMPLE AS THAT!

AAARR-GHHH! I LOVE HER!

IS SHE AN ANGEL?! NO ONE'S THIS NICE!
I WAS TRYING TO ACT COOL, BUT MAYBE I OVERDID IT...?
AUGH! SHE'S BLUSHING! WHAT A CUTIE!

WAIT, WHY AM I GUSHING OVER SOME HUMAN?!
I'M HONEY TRAP! AN EVIL KAIJIN! IF I NEED HELP FROM A HERO, I'M DOING SOMETHING WRONG!!

UH!
HMPH!
FWP
JUST BECAUSE YOU WERE A TEENSY BIT KIND TO ME, DON'T LET IT GO TO YOUR HEAD!
UM, OKAY?

I'LL SEE MYSELF OUT.
SHWP
STOMP
STOMP
CARE-FUL, HONEY-SAN!
AH!
HUH?
EEK!
BOMF

GYAAAH!
EEEK!!
STOP.
EH?

DON'T PUSH YOUR-SELF! STAY HERE FOR A LITTLE WHILE.

I'LL...
KEEP YOU SAFE.

HUH...?
I CAN STAY HERE...?

Ba-thump
THAT MEANS WE'D BE...

Ba-thump
SHACKING UP!
Ba-thump
Ba-thump

Ba-thud
Ba-thud
Ba-thud
WE'D BE LIVING IN SIN!!!
Ba-thud
Ba-thud
Ba-thud

OH!

OH
HO
HO
HO
HO
HO!

H-
HONEY-
SAN?
Shwp

WAH!
HMPH!
Tump

Ka-shink

POW!
WHOA! WHAT THE --?!

Clink
YOU, MY DEAR, ARE *TERRIBLY* NAIVE!

Slide
Swish
H-HONEY-SAN?
WHY'D YOU CHANGE YOUR APPEARANCE?
WHY ELSE?
IT'S A DISGUISE FOR LIVING IN HUMAN SOCIETY.
Shuuu
DONE!
THIS WILL SUFFICE.
AND...
TO GET PAYBACK AT THAT TOXIC EVIL ORGANIZATION THAT TOSSED ME AWAY.
Shi-ne
!
REALLY ?!
YES.

I'VE PUT MY VILLAIN-OUS DAYS BEHIND ME.
ALLOW ME TO INTRODUCE MYSELF PROPERLY. MY NAME'S HONEY TRAP.

THE PLEASURE IS ALL MINE!
RAPID RABBIT, AT YOUR SER-VICE!
OH! BUT MY REAL NAME IS HONJO HAYATE!

HAPPY TO WORK WITH YOU, HONEY-SAN!
LIKEWISE, HAYATE-SAN!

WAIT, SO YOU HAD A REAL NAME ALL ALONG?
HONEY-SAN IS YOUR ACTUAL NAME...?
OH HO HO! YES, IT IS.

Shuf...
I HAVE A REPORT, X-SAMA.
IT SEEMS HONEY TRAP HAS TEAMED UP WITH RAPID RABBIT.

......
GOOD WORK.
Shff

FWOOSH
WHAT DO YOU INTEND TO DO?

NOTHING.
Pat

SO WHAT IF WE'RE SHORT ONE EX-ECUTIVE OFFICER?
ALL WE NEED TO DO IS FOLLOW THE PLAN, SAME AS BEFORE.

I DO HOPE THEY'LL ENTERTAIN ME.
I'LL ENJOY WATCHING THEM STRUGGLE.

RMMMMBLE
HEH HEH HEH HEH HEH HEH HEH HEH!
MWA HA HA HA HA HA HA HA HA HA HA HA!!!!

HA--
DON'T BE SO COCKY. LOSING AN EXECUTIVE OFFICER IS A HUGE BLOW!
Freeze

Turn
......

I KNOO-OOOW!!! WHEN I SAID SHE WAS FIRED, IT WAS JUST A JOKE!!!
Bwaaah!
THEN WHY SEND ASSAS-SINS?
I WAS ONLY GONNA HAVE THEM HALF-KILL HER BEFORE BRING-ING HER BACK HOME! GOD!
SERI-OUSLY ...?

BLAARGH! AND I WAS SO FOND OF HONEY-CHAN TOO! SHE HAD BIGGER BOOBS THAN YOU.
YOU WANT A FIGHT?
AND SO...

THE BATTLE BETWEEN MANKIND AND THE ANTINOIDS ENTERED A NEW ERA.

BAM
BAM
!!
OUTTA?!!

Klak
Ga-chak

TRANS-FORM UP!!
Sha
keen
THE SUPER-HERO-INE...

ZRR
TRANS-FORM ON...!
AND THE EX-VILLAIN-ESS.
ZRR

FLASH

OOO
OOO
OOO
OOO
VMM
THEIR STORY BEGINS HERE.

Meta Warrior
Superwomen in Love!
Honey Trap & Rapid Rabbit
Character Data

SUPERWOMEN
IN
LOVE!
HONEY TRAP & RAPID RABBIT

Chirp
Chirp
Chirp

Blink...
NN.

GOOD MORNING, HONEY-SAN!

HOW'D YOU SLEEP?
Sparkle

!!!!
Bluuush
UWAH?! HONEY-SAN, ARE YOU OKAY?!

CHAPTER 2 GETTING TO KNOW YOU
Z z z...

LOOK AT HER PERFECT FACE.
POP
THIS HAS BEEN AN EYE-OPENER.
I DIDN'T EXPECT A HERO'S LIFE TO BE SO NORMAL.
WELL, I AM JUST A NORMAL PERSON.
WHAT NORMAL PERSON TRANSFORMS INTO A HERO WITH A SPECIAL BRACELET?
O-OKAY, GOOD POINT.
QUITE A CURIOUS DEVICE... WHERE EXACTLY DID YOU GET IT?
SHWEEEN
OH, THIS?
I FOUND IT AT THE SHOPPING MALL IN THE NEXT TOWN OVER BY COMPLETE COINCIDENCE!!
Eh heh!
WHAT AN UNINSPIRED WAY TO BECOME A SUPER-HERO!!!

BUT...
OTHER THAN BEING RAPID RABBIT, HAYATE-SAN IS AN ORDINARY HUMAN.
DARK COFFEE
HERO MILK
AND IF I HAD TO SAY, A VERY CUTE ONE!
AND SEXY.

......
Dribble Dribble Dribble
ドボドボドボドボドボドボドボ

OH!
HEY, HONEY-SAN?
DWAH ?!
SHWP

Y-Y-YES?
SOME MORE INFO COULD BE REALLY USEFUL FOR FUTURE FIGHTS!
WOULD YOU MIND ANSWERING SOME QUESTIONS?
FWAOOOSH
YOU WANT TO KNOW ABOUT ME?!!
HERO MILK
Tnk

HAYATE-SAN! YOU'RE BOLDER THAN YOU LOOK!
Wah
Wah
OH, I MEANT ...
INFO ON THE ANTINOID ORGANIZATION, NOT YOU PERSONALLY.

FIRST OF ALL, THE ORGANIZATION HAS A LEADER, AND THREE EXECUTIVE OFFICERS OTHER THAN MYSELF.
THEN THERE ARE THE ARTIFICIALLY CREATED WEAPON KAIJIN, AND THE FOOT SOLDIERS.

IT'S LIKE THIS.
AHA, I SEE! SO I SHOULD BE EXTRA CAREFUL OF THOSE KAIJIN AND THEIR POWERS!
KAIJIN
HAVE UNIQUE APPEARANCES AND SPECIAL POWERS. STRONGER, BUT MORE COSTLY.
META WARRIORS
SOLDIERS. CAN BE PRODUCED AT LOW COST, BUT WEAK.

TA-DA
HMM. IT'D BE ROUGH IF I EVER FACED TWO OF THEM AT ONCE...
GAH!
OH.
DON'T WORRY. IT'LL NEVER HAPPEN.
WHY IS THAT?

THE EXTRA COST COMES OUT OF OUR PAY.
ONLY THIS MUCH FOR THE MONTH...?
Alien Bank
TIMES ARE TOUGH !!

NEXT, THE EXECUTIVE OFFICERS. FIRST, THERE'S MELT OUT, A MAD SCIENTIST-- "MAD" AS IN SHE'S GRUMPY ALMOST ALL THE TIME.
A MAD SCIENTIST, EH? I GUESS EVERY EVIL ORGANIZATION'S GOTTA HAVE ONE!
NEXT IS SUIGETSU KYOKA. SHE'S VISITED THE HUMANS' WORLD SEVERAL TIMES TO DO RECON-NAISSANCE.
SHE'S AN ODD ONE, ALWAYS GOING ON ABOUT *BUSHIDO* OR SOME-THING.
HM! SO THEY HAVE SPIES, TOO!
AS FOR THE LAST ONE... NOT ONLY DO THEY RARELY SHOW UP, WE'VE BARELY SPOKEN, SO I'VE GOT NOTHING.
YOUR EXPLANA-TIONS ARE GETTING SLOPPY!

FINALLY, THERE'S THE ANTINOID LEADER, X.
SHE'S GARBAGE.
THE MEANEST EXPLANATION YET, AND IT'S FOR THE BOSS!!!!

HOW DARE THAT DAMN WOMAN TRY TO TERMINATE *ME?* BAILING WAS THE RIGHT DECISION. UNBELIEVABLE...
GRR
GRR
GRR
GNAW GNAW GNAW
I ALMOST FEEL SORRY FOR THE BOSS.

AHEM!
BUT ENOUGH ABOUT HER.
HAYATE-SAN, I'D LIKE TO ASK YOU SOME QUESTIONS, TOO!
Fwip
OKAY?
WHAT ARE YOUR HOBBIES ...?
IS THIS A MARRIAGE INTERVIEW?!
UM!
I LIKE WATCHING SUPER-HERO SHOWS, I GUESS? KINDA CUZ I'M ONE MYSELF.
← The type who'll answer anyway.
ALSO, I OCCASIONALLY WORK GIGS AS AN EMCEE FOR HERO SHOWS!
REALLY?! I MUST WATCH ONE OF YOUR SHOWS SOMETIME!

ACK! YOU CAN'T!
GAAAH!
WH-WHY-EVER NOT?!

ERR!
THE OUTFIT IS SUPER FRILLY AND KINDA REVEALING.
I DON'T WANT SOMEONE I KNOW TO SEE ME IN IT...

SHE PERFORMS IN SUCH SCANDAL-OUS ATTIRE?!
※ Mental image

I'M GOING TO THAT SHOW IF IT'S THE LAST THING I DO!
BIP BIP BIP
AH!

WHAT'S THAT ALARM?
IT ALERTS ME WHEN A KAIJIN'S NEARBY!
CONVE-NIENT!

SORRY, HONEY-SAN!
I'VE GOT TO GO.
BAM

SO FAST!!
VWOOM
DO YOU ALWAYS RUN TO THE SCENE ON FOOT?!

AH! MY DEAR! DON'T LEAVE ME BEHIND!
I'LL GO WITH YOUUU!!!

NOOOO!!
OOOOOOO
EW! I'M STUCK!
OO
ANTINOID KAIJIN
CLING ANTINOID
GLUES EVERYTHING TOGETHER WITH THE POWER OF A UNIQUE SUBSTANCE!
BAM
?!
THAT'S FAR ENOUGH, ANTI-NOID!!

VWIP
FULL OF COUR-AGE!

FLASH
FULL SPEED AHEAD!

RAPID RABBIT HAS ARRIVED !!
BAM
BA-
I'LL PROTECT THIS SCHOOL !!

VOOSH
HYAAAAH!
THAK
THAK
THAK
THAK
THAK
THAK
GA-
WHAM!
TMP
WHOA!
HOP
OUTTA!
VOOOM

AH!
EEEK!
NOT GOOD! IF WE FIGHT HERE, THESE INNOCENT PEOPLE WILL BE DRAGGED INTO IT!
YOU STAY...
TMP TMP TMP TMP
AWAY FROM THEM!
KA-CLASH
Sneer
Twist...
SPLURT
WHAT ?!

Creak
HUFF!
I FINALLY CAUGHT UP.
GOOD GRIEF! THAT GIRL...
SHE JUST HAD TO TAKE OFF ON HER OWN.
Clak
UWAAAAH
HM?
GBFF!
BLAM

UWAA-
AAH!!
KTHWAAM

WH...
KOFF
WHAT IS GOING ON HERE?!
KOFF

Squuuish

WHA?!
HAWAH, WAH, WAH, WAH, WAAAH!!!
OW!

HONEY-SAN? WHAT ARE YOU DOING HERE?
I WAS ABOUT TO ASK YOU THAT!!!

WAIT, WHAT IS THIS?! I'M STUCK!
IS THIS THAT KAIJIN'S ABILITY?!
Squirm
Squirm
WE NEED TO GET OUT OF THIS GOOP, FAST!
AH!
SEEMS SO!
Squirm
Squirm
......
HONEY-SAN?

ドキドキドキドキドキドキドキドキドキドキ
BA-THUMP BA-THUMP BA-THUMP BA-THUMP BA-THUMP
I CAN'T FOCUS ON WHAT SHE'S SAYING WHEN SHE'S SO CLOSE TO ME!

I'M SORRY. THIS IS ALL MY FAULT.

YOU HAVE EVERY RIGHT TO BE ANGRY.

I LED THE BAD GUYS RIGHT TO YOU.
AND AFTER YOU FINALLY LEFT THAT LIFE BEHIND.

IT'S...
SO *HARD* TO PROTECT THE PEOPLE YOU CARE ABOUT.

YES.
I'M QUITE CROSS IN-DEED.

BUT!
ONLY BECAUSE YOU STILL DON'T *TRUST* ME!
HRMPH!

HON...
HONEY-SAN?
Glare

TAKING OFF ALONE LIKE THAT BEFORE I COULD EVEN GET A WORD IN!
DO YOU REALLY THINK YOU HAVE TO TAKE EVERY-THING ON ALONE?

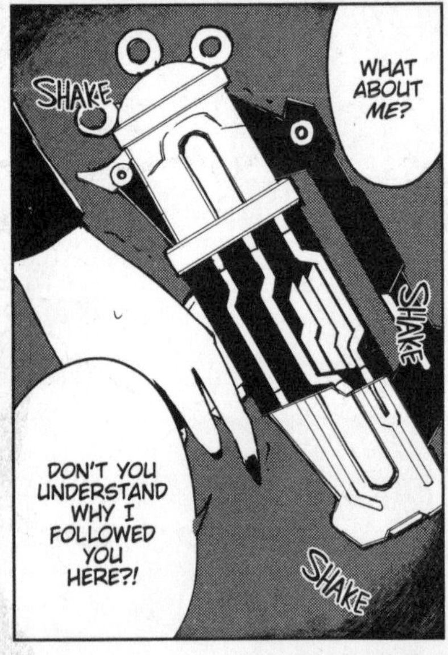
WHAT ABOUT ME?
SHAKE
SHAKE
DON'T YOU UNDERSTAND WHY I FOLLOWED YOU HERE?!
SHAKE

WHEN I TEAMED UP WITH YOU, I MEANT I WANTED TO FIGHT ALONGSIDE YOU!!
Gasp!

AH!
I-I MEAN ...!
Flail
Flail

I'VE DEFEATED YOU ONCE BEFORE! YOU *KNOW* I CAN HOLD MY OWN IN A FIGHT!
LET'S GO FROM BEING ENEMIES TO PARTNERS! WELL? WHAT DO YOU SAY?
HONEY-SAN...

Grin
ALL RIGHT!
PLEASE LEND ME A TEENSY BIT OF YOUR STRENGTH!
Beam
OH HO HO!
Ka-chak
GLADLY. ♪
BLAM
OH!
Tap
!

Click
Click
TRANS-FORM UP!!
TRANS-FORM ON!!
SHA-KEEN
VVVUH!
FLASH

A HERO ALWAYS ENDS THINGS WITH A SPECIAL MOVE!
FIRST STEP!
HOW AMUSING. ALL RIGHT, I'LL PLAY ALONG.
HUP!
VSH

RAPID STOMP!!
HAZE SHOT!!
Outta way!!
KA-BWAAAM

PAA-
CRACK

H-HUH?
WHAT IS THIS STUFF ...?
WHAT WERE WE JUST DOING...?

SHUMMM...
THAT'S A WRAP!
INDEED.
HONEY-SAN.
?
SW
OOP
WAH!
H-HAYATE-SAN?!
WHAT...

THANKS SO MUCH FOR YOUR HELP TODAY!!
Smile

Twiiinge
H-HAYATE-SAN...♡

I CAN DIE HAPPY NOW.
UWAH! HONEY-SAN?!
Diiing
......
Chak
EXPERIMENT COMPLETE.
OKAY.
WE'RE DONE HERE, KYOKA.

HONEY-SAN, I REALLY THINK THIS IS TOO CRAMPED...
APARTMENTS
I STILL DON'T UNDERSTAND *WHY* YOU THINK WE SHOULD SHARE THE BED!
SQUEEZE

IS THAT A PROB-LEM?
WE'RE FRIENDS NOW, SO...

BESIDES, I CAN'T POSSIBLY IMPOSE ON YOU AND KEEP THE BED TO MYSELF.
YOU WON'T GET A FULL NIGHT'S REST ON THE FLOOR.
HONEY-SAN... DID YOU SUGGEST THIS FOR MY SAKE?

NOPE! IT'S JUST AN EXCUSE TO GET CLOSER TO HER!
Geh heh
THE PERFECT PLAN, IF I DO SAY SO MYSELF! THOUGH I MUST ADMIT MY HEART'S POUNDING SO HARD I MIGHT DIE.
heh heh heh heh!

HEE HEE!
WHAT'S SO FUNNY?
?

IT'S FUN, SLEEPING TOGETHER LIKE THIS!
Eh hee hee!
LIKE A COUPLE! HEH!

A COUPLE ?!!

GOOD NIGHT, SLEEP TIGHT, HONEY-SAN!
Doze...
Stare
Stare
Stare
A COUPLE... A COUPLE... A COUPLE...
Stare
Stare
Stare
SHE DIDN'T GET A WINK OF SLEEP THAT NIGHT.

Cling Antinoid (Kaijin)
Superwomen in Love!
Honey Trap & Rapid Rabbit
Character Data

SUPERWOMEN
IN
LOVE!
HONEY TRAP & RAPID RABBIT

DEAR FOOLISH, VACATION-LESS ANTI-NOIDS...
HERE, HAYATE-SAN!
FOR YOU!
Sparkle
Paid

AWW! THANKS, HONEY-SAN!
OH, NO NEED TO THANK ME! ♡

Chomp
SO SWEET! ♡

EVER SINCE I LEFT THE ORGANI-ZATION, I, HONEY TRAP, HAVE BEEN LEADING MY BEST LIFE!!
HIFF! HIFF! HIFF!
HIFF!
YOU'RE SWEET!
HIFF!
HIFF!

CHAPTER 3 ENCOUNTER & REUNION

OH HO HO!
I FEEL MY BOND WITH HAYATE-SAN DEEPENING EVERY DAY!
IN FACT, IT'S LIKE WE'RE ON A DATE RIGHT NOW!
Nom
Nom

NOT TO MENTION ...
"LIKE A COU-PLE!"
Sl...igh!

IS IT ONLY A MATTER OF TIME BEFORE THAT'S TRUE?
Heh Heh Heh
?
30..300.
PAID

THIS IS A NEW SIDE TO YOU, HONEY TRAP.

Ah!
IT CAN'T BE...
MELT OUT?!
Swish
GOOD TO SEE YOU, TOO.
SOME-ONE YOU KNOW?
Chew
OH, I KNOW HER ALL RIGHT.
SHE'S ONE OF THE EXECUTIVE OFFICERS I TOLD YOU ABOUT.
ZRRR
ZRRR
WHA?! HER?!
ANTINOID EXECUTIVE OFFICER
MELT OUT

I REMEMBER NOW.
YOU SAID SHE'S A MAD SCI-ENTIST, RIGHT?
QUITE.
MELT OUT PRODUCES NUMER-OUS ITEMS WE CALL DIMENSION TOOLS.
THE ANTI D-BUSTER I USE TO TRANS-FORM? SHE BUILT THAT.
AT ANY RATE, SHE'S A DANGER-OUS WOMAN.
Gulp...
WHAT'S SOMEONE LIKE THAT DOING HERE?
UNTIL WE KNOW HER OBJECTIVE, I HAVE TO HIDE MY IDENTITY AS A HERO!
Fidget
Fidget
OH.
Sneer

SO YOU'RE RAPID RABBIT, HMM?
JOLT
GAH!
N-NO!
Y-Y-Y-YOU'VE GOT THE WRONG GIRL! RAPID RABBIT?! NEVER HEARD OF HER!!
Wave
Wave
Wave
Wave
SHE'S A TERRIBLE LIAR...

Secret Identity Unknown!
Gloom
SO?
WHAT'S A BUSY OFFICER LIKE YOU DOING HERE?
DID YOU COME TO FINISH ME OFF?

Glare
HOW STUPID.
YOU KNOW YOU'RE NO MATCH FOR THE BOTH OF US.

NAH. I'M OFF TODAY. I'M NOT HERE FOR A FIGHT.
JUST HAPPENED TO BUMP INTO YOU.
Meh!
SO EVEN VILLAINS GET DAYS OFF...?

WELL, THAT'S A RELIEF! RIGHT, HONEY-SA...
Phew!

HONEY-SAN?!
THUD
Day... off?

IMPOSSIBLE! THE BOSS WORKS HER EMPLOYEES TO THE BONE! BUT YOU GET TO TAKE A VACATION?!
SHAKE
SHAKE

I MADE A KAIJIN TO DEMAND VACATION DAYS FROM X.
PEACE!
Ker-smack
CLOAK LADY SUCK
MORE DAYS OFF!
SO CRUEL... BUT BRIL-LIANT!!!
ANTI-TOXIC BOSS KAIJIN
STRIKE ANTINOID

I SEE YOU'RE AS UNDER-HANDED AS EVER, MELT.
Heh!
YOU SAY THAT LIKE IT'S A BAD THING.
I'LL DO WHAT-EVER WILL GET ME RESULTS.

HEY! IF YOU'RE NOT HERE TO FIGHT, THEN GET LOST!!
GRRR!
Blunt
NO.
I'M MEETING SOME-ONE HERE.
MEETING WHO EXACTLY?
?

OH, YOU KNOW HER QUITE WELL.
Heh heh heh...
SURELY YOU RE-MEMBER SUIGETSU KYOKA?

!
SHE'S COMING TOO?!

HONEY-SAN! ISN'T SUIGE-TSU...?
RIGHT.
ANOTHER EXEC-UTIVE OFFICER, JUST LIKE MELT.

SHE'S BEEN OPERATING IN THIS WORLD EVEN LONGER THAN ME.
SHE OFTEN TEAMS UP WITH MELT TO PULL STRINGS BEHIND THE SCENES.

WOW, THEY MEET UP EVEN ON THEIR DAYS OFF? THEY SOUND CLOSE~!
AWW!
AWW!
IT'S NOT CUTE AT ALL!
GAAAH!

...!
SHE'S A COLD-BLOODED SWORDS-WOMAN!
Gulp
IF SHE SEES AN ENEMY, SHE'LL ATTACK MERCI-LESSLY.

AH.
!

YOU CALLED?

Ugh!
SUIGE-TSU KYOKA!

OTAKU!
UH, WHO IS SHE?!!!
I SAY, THIS TOWN'S SHOPS ARE OVER-FLOWING WITH DESIRABLE GOODS~!
DWUUUH? LONG TIME NO SEE, COMRADE HONEY~!
Uhhh?
WHAT DID SHE JUST CALL ME?!

AH!
HONEY-SAN! SHE ISN'T HOW YOU DESCRIBED HER AT ALL!
Bwhaaa?
I'VE NEVER SEEN THAT OTAKU BEFORE IN MY LIFE!
WHO IS THAT GIRL?!
?
THAT'S KYOKA.
WHAT ARE YOU TALKING ABOUT?
ARE YOU SURE?!

ACTUALLY, I *DO* SEE SOME SWORDS.
THOSE ARE JUST GLOW STICKS!!
I CAN'T GET OVER HOW MUCH YOU'VE CHANGED!!
WHAT HAPPENED?!
Shake
Shake

AH, OF COURSE. YOU'VE NEVER SEEN ME IN THIS FORM BEFORE.
I'LL CHANGE.
SHWP
Erk!

デュフフーン!!
Deh hehheh!!
TA-DA! QUICK CHANGE COMPLETE!!
YES, IT IS I, SUIGETSU KYOKA!
ANTINOID EXECUTIVE OFFICER SUIGETSU KYOKA
I MUST CONFESS, EVEN SINCE MY ARRIVAL IN THIS WORLD, I'VE BEEN LIVING THE LIFE OF A HERMIT, SETTLED IN THE SAME PLACE LIKE SOME KIND OF MOSS. BEFORE I KNEW IT, I'D BECOME WHAT YOU SAW BEFORE YOU...
Mutter
Mutter
Mutter
Sprout
Sprout
Sprout
SHE'S REALLY GONE ALL IN, EH?
SHE'S BEYOND HELP.
ARE YOU GOING TO ALLOW THIS, MELT?!
MM?
LOOK WHAT'S BECOME OF YOUR PARTNER!!
Glance
MEH.
NOTHING EVER FAZES HER!

AH! WOULD THAT LOVELY LASS THERE BE RAPID RABBIT?
Gyoooh!
BUSTED AGAIN ?!
WELL, YES. BECAUSE YOU'RE WITH ME.
Smirk

I SEE. SO YOU ARE COMRADE HONEY'S TYPE?
Leer
HAVE YOU MADE IT TO FIRST BASE YET?
Smirk
GAH!

IDIOT!! HOW DARE YOU!!
HEY! STOP IT! I'LL GO BALD!
RIP
RIP
RIP
HER MUSH-ROOMS ARE GETTING RIPPED OUT...
FUN FACT, THEY'RE EDIBLE.
YOU EAT THEM ?!

WAIT!
RIP
RIP

YOU'VE CHANGED A LOT YOURSELF, COMRADE HONEY!

YOU HATED THE HUMANS MORE THAN ANY OF US. WHY ARE YOU PROTECTING THEM?!

WHY INDEED?
WE ARE LIFE-FORMS OUT TO DESTROY MANKIND.
TRYING TO PROTECT ONE? IT SIMPLY ISN'T IN OUR NATURE.

BUT I CAN DO IT.
LOOM

D
BECAUSE I'M IN LOVE!
UN
COME AGAIN?
DU.
BECAUSE I'M IN LOVE WITH A HERO!
DUUN
ERR, THAT DOESN'T EXPLAIN ANY-THING...
WITH LOVE, ANYTHING IS POSSIBLE!
"HONEY-SAN!"
SHE MAKES ME BELIEVE IT.
AND SHE CALLED ME BEYOND HELP?
ho ho Oh ho ho!

BUT NO MATTER.

I'M ON A DATE.
I DON'T HAVE TIME TO PLAY WITH YOU TWO.
FWI
Sh
THAT SO?

Shwp

TELL ME ONE THING BEFORE WE PART.
WHAT ...?

Twitch
I WANT TO KNOW ABOUT THAT BRACELET ON HER WRIST.
......

I SEE.
SO THAT'S RAPID RABBIT'S TRANSFORMATION ITEM.
I ALSO THOUGHT IT ODD MYSELF.

DON'T YOU FIND IT STRANGE, HONEY TRAP?
ORDINARY HUMANS DON'T RETAIN MEMORIES RELATED TO US ANTI-NOIDS.
WHAT IS THIS STUFF?

YET THAT HUMAN... RAPID RABBIT... HER MEMORIES REMAIN INTACT.

SO YOU DO KNOW SOMETHING!
NAH.
NEVER SEEN IT BEFORE.

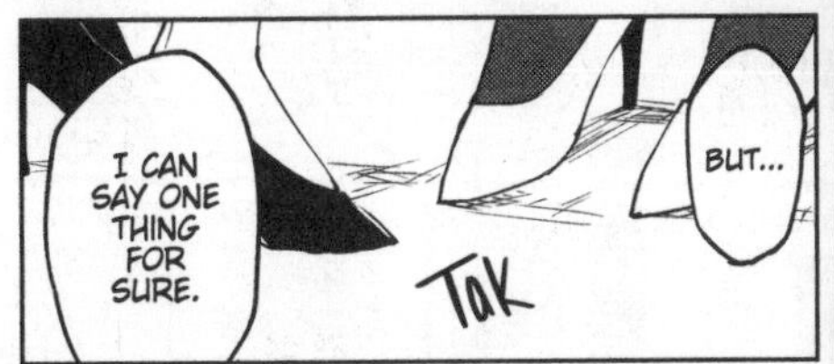
BUT...
I CAN SAY ONE THING FOR SURE.
TAK

THAT'S A DIMENSION TOOL.
SHIVER
WHA...
WATCH YOUR-SELF.
WE'LL WITH-DRAW... FOR NOW.
TIME TO GO, KYOKA.
Stride
Stride
Stomp
H-HEY! WAIT FOR ME, COMRADE MELT~!!
Stomp

THEY'RE FRIENDLIER THAN I WAS EXPECTING!
Aww!
THEY ARE THE ENEMY!!
THEY'D KILL YOU AND ALL OF HUMAN-KIND!!
OH YEAH! I FOR-GOT!!
SHE'S TOO PURE FOR THIS WORLD.
HEY, WHAT WERE YOU TALKING ABOUT WITH THEM BACK THERE?
IT...
WAS NOTHING.
......
30R
300R
P
Paid

HEY, COMRADE MELT.
WHITE.

Cliiing
MUST YOU CLING SO TIGHTLY?!

AM NOT...

AHA! I SEE!

DID YOU GROW JEALOUS UPON SEEING COMRADE HONEY ON A DATE?
Shift
THAT'S NOT...!

YAK
BUT REGRETTABLY, I HAVE ANIME TO BINGE, FIGURES TO OPEN AND PLAY WITH, A NEW DATING SIM WITH ROUTES I MUST FULLY CONQUER, AND MANY MORE THINGS I MUST DO~!
YAK
YAK
YOU DON'T SOUND LIKE A KAIJIN OUT TO DESTROY THE HUMAN RACE.
NOW, I SHALL WATCH ANIME!
Swup
Slip
AH!

......
DON'T YOU EVER...
UM!
WANT TO GO TO THEME PARKS, OR ON A TRIP...OR ANYTHING?
Creak

BLUNT
NOPE!
THAT WAS QUICK!

SITTING ON MY BUTT WATCHING ANIME, LOOKING UP FIGURES' SKIRTS, AND PLAYING TONS OF DATING SIMS TO MASTERY...
SPROUT SPROUT
Deh heh heh heh!
'TIS TOO MUCH FUN!
R-REALLY?

Mm?
WOULDN'T YOU HAVE BETTER FOCUS ALONE, THEN?

WRONG AGAIN.

AFTER ALL...
SUCH THINGS ARE FUN BECAUSE YOU ARE THERE WITH ME!
Grin

AH!
WHERE DID *THAT* COME FROM?!
OHO!
ARE YOU BLUSH-ING?!
I'M NOT!
MUSH-ROOMS FOR DINNER TODAY!
HOLD IT! WHERE ARE THOSE FROM?!

Strike Antinoid (Kaijin)
Superwomen in Love!
Honey Trap & Rapid Rabbit
Character Data

SUPERWOMEN
IN
LOVE!
HONEY TRAP & RAPID RABBIT

Dance Mask
Hero Show
Venue
THANKS FOR COMING TO OUR HERO SHOW!!
HELLO, EVERY-BODY!!
YAY!
HELLOOO!!
わぁ WO あO!
あっ

CHAPTER 4: SHOWTIME STARTS SUDDENLY

OKAY, LET'S ALL CALL FOR THEM TOGETHER!
IT'S DIFFERENT THAN HER USUAL STYLE, BUT SHE LOOKS FANTASTIC IN THIS, TOO!
SO...
CUUUTE!! OH, HAYATE-SAN!!

OH HO HO! I KNOW HAYATE-SAN SAID NOT TO COME BECAUSE SHE WAS TOO EMBARRASSED...
MASK RANGER!
Clench!
BUT COMING IN SECRET WAS ABSOLUTELY THE RIGHT DECISION!

Flu
ttter
ISN'T THAT SKIRT TOO SHORT THOUGH?
BEND A LITTLE AND YOU COULD TOTALLY SEE UNDER IT.

AHHH! JUST A LITTLE MORE AND I SHALL SEE IT~!

SPROUUUT
POP
POP
HRRRM! THEY'RE JUST BARELY OUT OF VIEW!
I THOUGHT AS MUCH. I SHALL HAVE TO SIT IN THE FRONT.

......
YAY!
WOOO!
HUH?

SNEEEAK
GRAB
AND WHERE MIGHT YOU BE GOING, KYOKA?
KRRK
KRRK
KRRK
OW, OW, OW, OW! STOP! STOP, COMRADE HONEY!!!

YEAH!
WOOO!
WELL?
YAY!

WHAT ARE YOU DOING HERE?
GL
ARE
IF LOOKS COULD KILL!

I SHOULD HOPE YOU AREN'T PLANNING TO SEND A KAIJIN INTO THE CROWD?
GRRK!

I KNEW IT!
WHERE'S MELT, THEN?
SHE'S, UH... HOLED UP IN THE LAB TODAY.
YOU DON'T SAY?

THAT MEANS...
YOU'RE HERE BY YOUR LONESOME?
Smirk...
Gah!
D-DRAT, I'VE SAID TOO MUCH!!

AT THIS RATE...
HERE I COME, NO-FACE!
I SHALL BE BEATEN LIKE A KAIJIN IN A HERO SHOW!!
ARRRGH!
KIIIN
EEEK!
Clench...
CURSES!
YOU LEAVE ME NO CHOICE!
SNAP
COME TO ME, META WARRIORS!!
NO! DON'T!

OUTTAWAAAY!!!
SAFETY FIRST
BAAAM
GUARD ANTINOID CAN BLOCK ANY ATTACK WITH ITS SHIELDS!

Gasp!

Murmur
HUH? WHO'S THAT?
SAFETY FIRST
COOL!
Murmur
IS THIS PART OF THE SHOW?

WHAT ARE THEY DOING HERE?!
ANTI-NOIDS?!

Psst!
HEY, WAS THAT IN THE SCRIPT?!
NO!
I'M SORRY, BUT PLEASE EVACUATE THE AUDIENCE!
ON IT!!

EVERYONE, GET OUT OF HERE!!
Eek!
GAAAH! WHY NOW OF ALL TIMES?!
CLACK
Eek!
CLACK
THE KIDS WERE LOOKING FORWARD TO THE SHOW!

WATCH OUT, CUZ I'M MAD NOW!
KIIIN
TRANS-FORM UP!!

KYO-KAAA!! YOU IDIOT!!!
ぎゅむぅ
Piiinch
H-HAN 'OO BLAME ME?!
UNGH!
I AM A VILLAIN! AND 'TIS NOT MY DAY OFF TODAY!
Eeeeeek!

TSK!
AND ON THE ONE DAY I CAN'T COME TO HAYATE-SAN'S RESCUE...
?
DID YOU HAVE A FIGHT OR SOME SUCH?
Sting Sting
WE WOULD NEVER FIGHT, OBVIOUSLY!!!
EEP!

YOU SEE...
HAYATE-SAN DOESN'T KNOW I WAS HERE WATCHING HER SHOW. SHE MIGHT GET CROSS WITH ME!
Wibble

HOW FORTUNATE FOR ME! WELL, PERHAPS I SHALL GO BOTHER RAPID RABBIT, THEN!
GRIN
WHA--! HOLD IT RIGHT THERE, KYOKA!
JOLT
CHAK
!
OH?
KASHK
ARE YOU GOING TO STOP ME, HONEY TRAP?
GAH...
......
GRR!
CHAK

TRANS-
FORM
ON!
POW!!
BOOF!
!
HON...
HONEY-
SAN?!
WHAT'S
SHE
DOING
HERE?!

H-HUH?!
WHAK
CLANG
SHING
CRING
SHOOT. I HAVE TO FOCUS ON *THESE* ENEMIES FIRST.
SHUFFLE
SHUFFLE
Wobble...
DEH HEH HEH!
Grr!
I THINK SHE SAW YOU, COMRADE HONEY!
NO THANKS TO YOU!!
WAH! CLOSE ONE!
BLAM
BLAM
BLAM
BLAM
BLAM
BLAM
BLAM
ANY-HOW...
THE KAIJIN OF THE DAY IS SUPPOSED TO BE ENHANCED BY MELT'S EXPERIMENT.
Dash

FULL OF COUR-AGE!
SHWOOM
GYURRRRR
FULL SPEED AHEAD!
KA-BLAM
RAPID RABBIT!!
SHAAA
GA
TUP

VWOM
I'LL PROTECT... THE KIDS' DREAMS!
FWSH
AH!
ALSO...
SHE'S STRONGER THAN I THOUGHT.
KA-BOOOM
COMRADE HONEY SEEMS ESPECIALLY ANGRY TODAY!!

HOW-EVER!
TUMP
I AM ALSO AN EXECUTIVE OFFICER, JUST AS YOU ONCE WERE!
FWOOSH
GAH!
SLASH
WHEN IT COMES TO ABILITY, WE'RE EVENLY MATCHED!!
HIYA!
THW
AM
SKSTHHH

DYU HU HU HU! DID YOU SEE THAT? THROUGH THE OTAKU ART OF GLOW STICK CHEERING, MY SWORDSMAN-SHIP HAS REACHED PERFECTION!!
VOOSH
VOOSH
NOW FOR THE FINISHING BLOW!
SHWOOOOO
GUH!
THMP
IT'S OVER, HONEY TRAP!!
SHWOOOSH
CLAAANG
OOOOO

SHUGYUUU
Ah!
SHE...
SHE STOPPED IT?!
BAIIM
OH, IT'S FAR FROM OVER.
CHK

AFTER ALL...
SHE AND I ARE JUST GETTING STARTED!
KA-SHUNK
SECOND STEP!!

DASH
RABBIT SMASH!!
BLAM

Krrak
SKREE
Outtaway!
BA
BWOOM
CLATTER
CLATTER
SWISH
Ah!
IS HONEY-SAN OKAY?!

SHUUUUUUUU

Peace♥

TK
WIP

LOOKS LIKE THIS WHOLE TIME, SOMEONE WAS PROTECTING *ME.*

Dance
Hero S
Venu
Canceled due to an accident

THANKS A BUNCH, HONEY-SAN! YOU WERE A BIG HELP!
BUT... WHAT WERE YOU DOING HERE?
ERK!

ACK!
I AM SO SORRY, HAYATE-SAN!!
I WAS SO CU-RIOUS ABOUT YOUR WORK, I HAD TO COME!
FWIP
HUH ?!
YOU DON'T HAVE TO BOW ABOUT IT...!
Huuuh?
EH?

YOU AREN'T MAD AT ME?
WELL, NO.
BUT IT'S NOT VERY NICE OF YOU TO WATCH WITHOUT TELLING ME!
HMPH!
THIS OUTFIT IS SERIOUSLY EMBARRASSING...
ERK! SORRY.

I DON'T WEAR THINGS LIKE THIS USU-ALLY.
SO HONESTLY, IT'S KIND OF A NICE CHANGE.
Rustle

BUT...
IT'S NOT "ME" AT ALL, IS IT?
......

?
WHAT DO YOU MEAN?
I THINK YOU LOOK POSITIVELY ADORABLE.

Bluuuush
......
HUH?

WHUH ?!
WH-WH-WH-WHAT ARE YOU SAYING, HONEY-SAN?!!
FLAIL
SHE'S BLUSHING! HOW RARE...AND CUUUUUTE!!
OOH...
FLAIL
FLAIL

SHOOP
NOT AT ALL!
YOU'RE HELP-ING ME! REALLY!

I STILL MUST APOLOGIZE.
I FEEL LIKE I'M MESSING UP YOUR FIGHTING STYLE.
AH!

I...

Rustle...
I ALWAYS FEEL ANXIOUS WHEN I FIGHT ALONE.
IT WAS A RELIEF TO KNOW YOU HAD MY BACK.

I WAS SO HAPPY TO SEE YOU OUT THERE, FIGHTING ON THE SAME SIDE AS ME!
YOU WERE SO COOL, LIKE THE HEROES I LOVE!

OH HO!
A HERO? THAT'S A STRANGE THING TO CALL *MOI*, A FORMER VILLAINESS!

EH HEH HEH!
I FORGOT!

WELL, READY TO HEAD HOME, HAYATE-SAN?
YEAH! I HOPE OUR NEXT SHOW DOESN'T GET INTERRUPTED...

NEXT TIME, I'LL OFFICIALLY INVITE YOU!

TWAK
FWOOP
AH.

GYAAAAH!!!
KRRRSH
HAYATE-SAN!!!
Ping
I SAW THEM!
WHITE!!

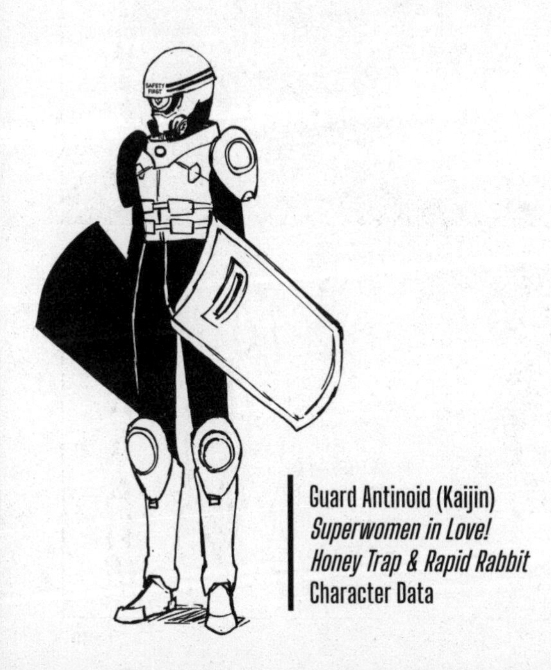

Guard Antinoid (Kaijin)
Superwomen in Love!
Honey Trap & Rapid Rabbit
Character Data

SUPERWOMEN IN LOVE!
HONEY TRAP & RAPID RABBIT

URRGH! PLEASE, HAVE MERCY!
SOOOB!

NO!
YOU MUST REFLECT ON YOUR FAILURE.
TAKA TAKA TAKA

SELLING HER FIGURE COLLECTION.
AND... SOLD! ♪
SHOCK
NOOOO!!!
WHAT ARE YOU TWO DOING?

CHAPTER 5 EMBRACE THE LOVE!

WAAAH! COMRADE MEEEELT !!!!
CL ING
WHAT'S WRONG, KYOKA? FAILED YOUR MISSION?

SHE CAME RUNNING BACK HERE AFTER GETTING HER BUTT KICKED! PATHETIC!
Fume
Fume
THERE, THERE.
Rub
Rub
YOU'RE ONE TO TALK.
I'M YOUR BOSS! SHOW SOME RESPECT!

X, FROM WHAT I CAN SEE, RAPID RABBIT AND HONEY TRAP ARE GROWING STRONGER EVERY DAY.
Rub
Rub
SHE IGNORED ME.
AT THIS RATE, THEY MAY USE *THAT* AGAINST US.
USE WHAT?

PERHAPS A NEW HERO OR A GIANT ROBOT.
*MENTAL IMAGE
ARE WE STILL TALKING ABOUT THE SAME THING?!
HEH! I'M KIDDING.
IT'S SO HARD TO TELL WITH YOU!

OOH, OOH! THEN WE'LL BREAK OUT THE GOOD STUFF TOO! MELT-CHAN, WE SHOULD TOTES USE YOUR NEW INVENTION IN OUR NEXT PLAN!
Plop
......
I NEVER SAID IT WAS FIN-ISHED.
OH? BUT YOU SEEM LIKE YOU'RE UP TO SOME-THING TODAY...
Heh heh...

SAW RIGHT THROUGH ME, DID YOU?
Smirk

OHO~! A NEW DIMENSION TOOL!
Slip...

Clink
THIS IS A NEW AND IMPROVED VERSION OF THE STIMULANT FOR BOOSTING LOW-LEVEL KAIJINS' STRENGTH.
I'LL USE IT ON THE NEXT KAIJIN WE CREATE.
THAT'S MY MAD SCIENTIST! YOU'RE ON A WHOLE 'NOTHER DIMENSION! HEH HEH.

THE ONLY THING IS...
ZZZ...
DAMMIT. WILL YOU WAKE UP, KYOKA?

NN ...?
Blink...
I NEED YOU TO GO WITH ME ON THE NEXT OPERATION.
WHAT?!
Boo!
WHY MUST I?! GO BY YOURSELF!
SORRY, BUT I'M NOT SUITED FOR COMBAT.
I'LL BE OBSERVING FROM AFAR.
FLAIL
FLAIL
GRRR!
FINE BY ME. CONSIDER IT A CHANCE TO REDEEM YOURSELF.
DON'T WORRY! WHEN YOU GET DEFEATED AND EXPLODE, I'LL FIND A REPLACEMENT FOR YOU!
Grin
MUST YOU SOUND SO CHEERFUL ABOUT IT?!

HOW VEXING! FINE! I SHALL GO ON THE MISSION!!
GRA-AAH!!
GOOD GIRL.
I'M SO PWOUD OF YOU, KYOKA-CHAN!!
DON'T BABY-TALK ME!!
Clap
Clap
Clap
Clap
Clap
Clap
Clap
Clap
Clap
Hmph!
CR
EEEAK
HEH HEH HEH.
I'LL BE EXPECTING SOME INTERESTING DATA.

THERE YOU ARE, ANTI-NOIDS!
DUN!
DUN!
RIDE ANTINOID ATTACKS WHILE RIDING A MOTORCYCLE!
WE WON'T LET YOU GET AWAY WITH THIS!
BAM!
ANTINOID KAIJIN!
AND...
HEH HEH!
KYO-KA-CHAN!
THAT MAKES IT SOUND LIKE WE ARE FRIENDS!!

OH! WAS THAT WEIRD?
FIRST THE BOSS DISRESPECTS ME, NOW YOU...
I JUST THOUGHT IT SOUNDED CUTE!
AH HA HA...
'TIS IMPORTANT TO MAINTAIN A SENSE OF FORMAL DISTANCE BETWEEN ENEMIES!!!
SHEESH!
EXACTLY, HAYATE-SAN!
WHY DO YOU CALL HER "CHAN" BUT ONLY USE "SAN" FOR ME?
Baaan
IS THAT THE PROBLEM?!
GONG
IN FACT, I'D LIKE YOU TO CALL ME "HONEY-CHAN" RIGHT NOW, EVEN IF IT'S ONLY ONCE!
Twinkle
HOW BOLD OF HER!
HRK!
UH... WELL, ERRR...
Twing
Twing

HON...
SHWOOO
Blushy
HONEY-CHAN...!
CAN I TELL YOU SOMETHING, HONEY-CHAN? I'VE ALWAYS... LOVED...
HONEY-CHAN!
HONEY-CHAN, HURRY UP!
HONEY-CHAN!
BOOM
HONEY-SAN?!
SHE'S LOST HER HEAD.

A-ANY-WAY!
WE CAN'T IGNORE YOUR EVIL DEEDS!
BAM!

I'LL PROTECT ...
KLAK
THIS TOWN'S PEACE!

CHAK
IS THAT SO?

SNAP
GA-SHUNK

VWSH
TRANS-
FORM
UP!
BLAM
TRANS-
FORM
ON!

VWEEL

SHIIING

AH!
T-TRANSFORM ON!
Chk
BWOOM
Shuuu...
NOW THEN...

Hyuuuu
YOU'LL BE DEALING WITH ME.
uuuu
OUTTA.

Va
Vrrrm
Dash
RAAAAH!
OOOOOOOO
Hyuu
IT DODGED?!
BAM
SCREEEETCH
TCH! PEST!
OUTTA-WAY!

I JUST NEED TO RECOVER MY BAL-ANCE...
Vrrrrrr
WHAM
GUH!
BAM
UGH!
HONEY-SAN!
VROOOO
DON'T LOOK AWAY FROM YOUR OPPONENT!
IT'S SO FAST!
Glint

FWWISSH
GAH!
OH MY! FOR A HERO CALLED "RAPID RABBIT," YOU'RE TERRIBLY SLOW, ARE YOU NOT?
KOFF!
DEH HEH HEH HEH!
NOW, TAKE THIS!
Twing
Wobble
SHRP
SHRP
SHRP

BA
SNAP
UWAH!
GRRRIP...
HEH!
I CAME UP WITH THIS TECHNIQUE FROM READING DOUJINSHI!
I SHALL POSE YOU LIKE ONE OF MY ANIME FIGURES!
UGH!
HAYATE-SAN!
Grrr...

Ah!
RM
RR
BR
OVER HERE, WEAK-LING!
Wave
SNAP
OUT-TA?!
BR
RR
OUTTA-WAAAY!
RRRM
HM?

BWA?!
WHAM
Screeech
NWAAAH!!!
GA-
SMAASH
Tump
G-GOT FREE...
Shw
GAAAH...
!
IT SEEMS YOU AND THAT KAIJIN AREN'T WORKING TOGETHER SO WELL.
STMP

AM
Pat
Pat
POWER ALONE ISN'T ENOUGH! YOU NEED LOVE!
IB
LIKE THE LOVE WE HAVE.
L...
LOVE?

YES!
EATING AND SLEEPING TOGETHER UNDER ONE ROOF!
FACING DOWN ENEMIES SIDE BY SIDE!
ONE MIGHT SAY WE'RE PRACTICALLY MARRIED!
ぱっ Fwip
THOSE ARE SOME BIG JUMPS YOU ARE MAKING!!
IT'S OKAY! HONEY-SAN CAN BE A LITTLE ECCENTRIC, BUT WE GET ALONG WELL!
So Pure
YOU CALL THAT A *LITTLE* ECCENTRIC?!

GRRR
DAMN YOU! HOW DARE YOU SHOVE YOUR NORMIE HAPPINESS IN MY FACE?!
Voosh
Ga-Shunk

HAZE BIND!!
SHOO
GEH!
BA-

NOW, HAYATE-SAN!!
HYUU
ON IT!
UH OH.
KIIN
FIRST STEP!!

KA-
RABBIT STOMP!!
KRAK
-Ba-
Gyaaa

KER-
WHAM
STMP

KRAK
UGH!

Shp
Shp
Clank
Clank
CURSES! I'M GONNA EXPLODE !!
BWAM

Wobble...
Shuuu...
PHEW! SAFE!

DOOOOOOM
......
OR NOT.

KAIJIN!
YOU HANDLE THIS--
ちーーーん
DIIING
KAI-JIIIIN!!!
Stomp
Flinch
W-WAIT! TIME OUT!
HAYATE-SAN, DON'T SHOW MERCY TO THIS DE-GENERATE.
NO, HOLD ON! I'LL APOLOGIZE FOR WHAT I'VE DONE, SO JUST WAIT!!
I'M STARTING TO FEEL SORRY FOR HER.

ACK!
A-APOLOGIES FOR PEEKING AT YOUR PANTIES LAST TIME, TOO!
YOU DID WHAT?!!
Bluuush
AH! CRAP!
'TWAS A SLIP OF THE TONGUE...

KYOKAAAA...
RUMBLE
WAAAAH!!!
C-COM-RADE MELT! SAVE MEEE!!!
EEEEK!
Tak
Heh.
PERFECT TIMING, KYOKA.
THE STIMULANT SHOULD KICK IN ANY MOMENT NOW.
Krik
Krak...
OUTTAWAY...

?!
CLATTER

?
WHAT ?!

THIS KAIJIN IS LIKE NOTHING THEY'VE FOUGHT BEFORE!

GO ON!
SHOW ME...
SWAY
OUTTA.
BA-
KRKKL
QUIVER
KRAK
KRAK
KRAK

THA-
THE POWER OF AN EVOLVED ANTINOID!
THOOOOM!

UM?
HONEY-SAN?
Y-YES, DEAR?
STARE...

YOU DON'T HAPPEN TO HAVE A GIANT ROBOT, DO YOU?
LIKE THIS?
THAT IS OUT OF THE BLUE. WHY DO YOU ASK?
Duun
JUST, HEROES TYPICALLY FIGHT THESE GIANT ENEMIES WITH ROBOTS, AND...
ゴゴゴ
RRRMBLE
I DON'T HAVE ANY-THING OF THE SORT!
VA-
VROM
WAAA-AAAH!!
THIS IS BAD!
IT'S HEADING INTO TOWN!
D P R R M R R
WH-WHAT'LL WE DO?! WE NEED TO STOP IT...

To be continued...

Ride Antinoid (Kaijin)
Superwomen in Love!
Honey Trap & Rapid Rabbit
Character Data

SUPERWOMEN
IN
LOVE!
HONEY TRAP & RAPID RABBIT

Superwomen in Love! Data File
Rapid Rabbit
Honey Trap
Suigetsu
Kyoka

RAPID RABBIT

Honjo Hayate's transformation using the R.R. Ring. It has armor called a "D-Frame," made of an extradimensional metal capable of redirecting impacts to another dimension. It's relatively lightweight and capable of temporary acceleration.

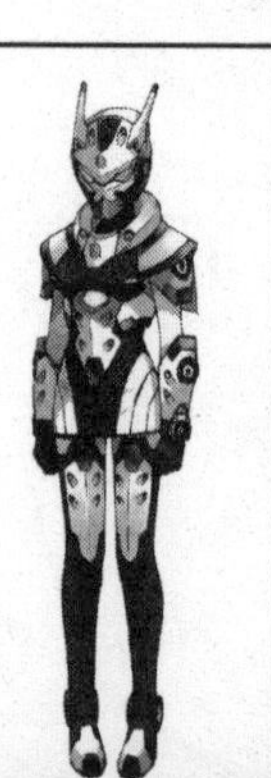

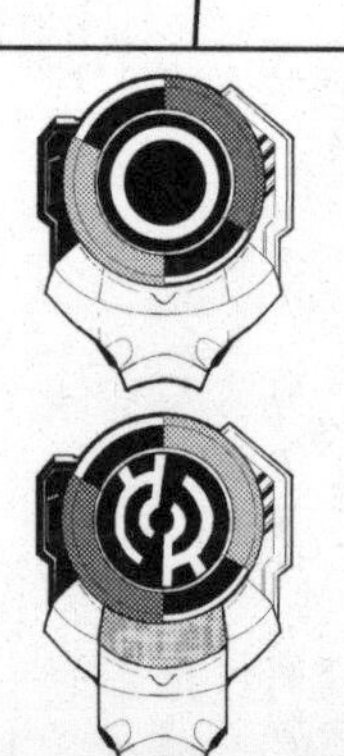

R.R. RING

The item Honjo Hayate uses when transforming into Rapid Rabbit. It might be an Antinoid dimension tool, but its origins are currently unknown.

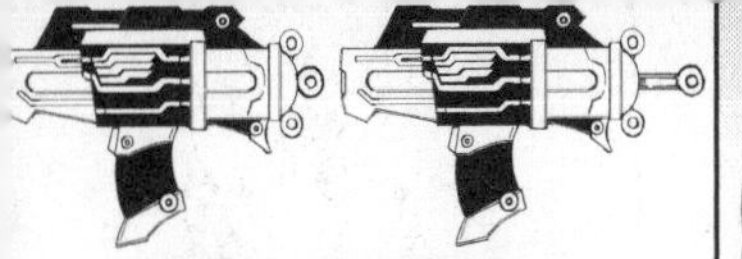

ANTI D-BUSTER

Standard equipment for Antinoid executive officers. By loading it with a different form, it can be used for transformation. Can also be used as a gun.

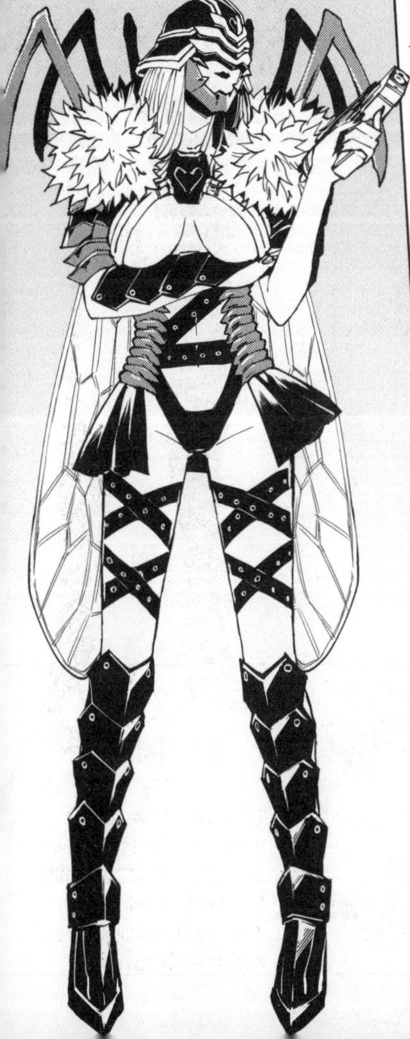

HONEY TRAP

Former Antinoid executive officer Honey Trap's true form. Though her physical abilities aren't very strong, she generates poison that can instantly kill most living creatures.

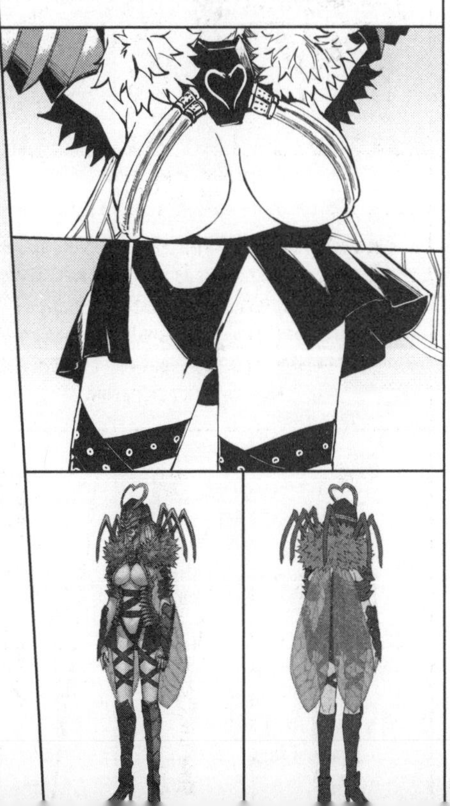

SUIGETSU KYOKA
One of the Antinoid executive officers. Mushrooms sprout from her head when she gets excited. When she's using her sword, her speed is on par with Rapid Rabbit's.
ANTI D-BUSTER
One of the dimension tools. When mortally wounded, it's possible to cheat death by using it to change into a new form.

SHORT: AFTER CHAPTER 1

SHORT: THE EXECUTIVE OFFICERS' MORNING

Chirp
Chirp
Chirp
Chirp
Chirp
Chirp
SNAP
BA-BAAAM
KYOKA RISES!!
FIRST THINGS FIRST! MUST DO DAILY QUESTS ON MY GAMES!
Lurch
HUH?

Drool~
WHAT IS IT, KYO-KAAA?
Ngh!
URGH!
I SUPPOSE I HAVE NO CHOICE!
I SHALL SLEEP A LITTLE LONGER, TOO!
Whump
Doze
YOU BETTER.
JUST TO BE CLEAR, THIS IS NOT YOUR HOME.
Turn

MEAN-WHILE IN THE HAYATE HOUSE-HOLD...
RISE AND SHINE, HONEY-SAN!
Twing
BWOOF
HER PERFECT FACE FIRST THING IN THE MORNING IS TOO MUCH!!!

SEVEN SEAS ENTERTAINMENT PRESENTS

SUPERWOMEN IN LOVE
HONEY TRAP & RAPID RABBIT

Vol. 1

story and art by **SOMETIME**

TRANSLATION
Amanda Haley

LETTERING
Mercedes McGarry

COVER DESIGN
Nicky Lim

LOGO DESIGN
George Panella

PROOFREADER
B. Lana Guggenheim

COPY EDITOR
Dawn Davis
Meg van Huygen

EDITOR
Shannon Fay

PREPRESS TECHNICIAN
Rhiannon Rasmussen-Silverstein

PRODUCTION ASSISTANT
Christa Miesner

PRODUCTION MANAGER
Lissa Pattillo

MANAGING EDITOR
Julie Davis

ASSOCIATE PUBLISHER
Adam Arnold

PUBLISHER
Jason DeAngelis

Seven Seas press and purchase enquiries can be sent to Marketing Manager Lianne Sentar at press@gomanga.com. Information regarding the distribution and purchase of digital editions is available from Digital Manager CK Russell at digital@gomanga.com.

ISBN: 978-1-64827-109-0
Printed in Canada
First Printing: April 2021
10 9 8 7 6 5 4 3 2 1

READING DIRECTIONS

This book reads from ***right to left***, Japanese style. If this is your first time reading manga, you start reading from the top right panel on each page and take it from there. If you get lost, just follow the numbered diagram here. It may seem backwards at first, but you'll get the hang of it! Have fun!!

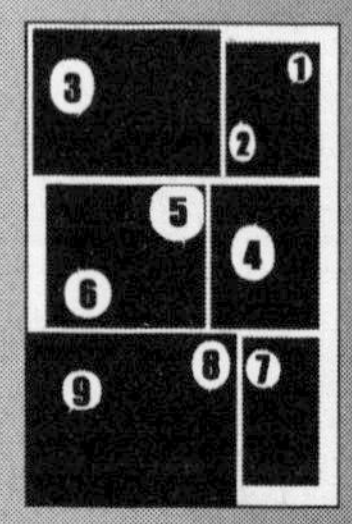

Follow us online: www.SevenSeasEntertainment.com